DEADLY DINOSAURS

Written by Rosie Rowntree

Illustrated by Marina Halak

First published in 2026 by Hungry Tomato Ltd
F15, Old Bakery Studios, Blewetts Wharf, Malpas Road, Truro, Cornwall,
TR1 1QH, UK.

A CIP catalog record for this book is available from the British Library.

ISBN 9781835696620

Manufactured in the USA

Discover more at
www.hungrytomato.com

HUNGRY
TOMATO®

CONTENTS

Words in **BOLD** can be found in the glossary.

THE WORLD OF DINOSAURS

Get ready to explore the wonderful world of dinosaurs! From the little Microraptor to the huge Allosaurus, there are so many different types of dinosaurs to discover.

WHAT WERE THE DINOSAURS?

Dinosaurs were a group of **reptiles** that lived on Earth millions upon millions of years ago. They ranged in size from the chicken-sized Compsognathus to the bus-sized Baryonyx. The word "dinosaur" comes from two Greek words meaning "terrible" and "lizard".

WHEN DID THE DINOSAURS LIVE?

Dinosaurs lived on Earth for almost 180 million years. But they didn't all live at the same time! Some were around later than others. Scientists think that the earliest dinosaurs first appeared over 245 million years ago, while the last roamed the Earth 66 million years ago.

WHAT HAPPENED TO THE DINOSAURS?

66 million years ago, a large **asteroid** hit Earth at incredibly high speed. It caused a lot of fires and sent huge waves crashing across the land. Dust from the asteroid affected the weather and reduced the amount of food that the dinosaurs had to eat.

This made most dinosaurs become **extinct** – except for those that could fly, which survived and developed into the birds that we are familiar with today!

Dinosaurs like confuciusornis looked a lot like birds!

An almost complete skeleton of T.rex has been found by scientists!

WHAT ARE FOSSILS?

Fossils are the remains of animals and plants that have been preserved for millions of years. They have been found on all seven of Earth's **continents**! Fossils of a dinosaur's entire **skeleton** are very rare. But even if they are found in bits and pieces, fossils allow scientists to learn a lot about the dinosaurs and their lives!

TYPES OF DINOSAURS

Scientists have arranged the dinosaurs into different categories based on things that they had in common, like their size or the way that they walked.

THEROPODS

Theropods all walked on two legs. Smaller theropods often had feathers, while larger ones were some of the biggest meat-eaters ever!

PACHYCEPHALOSAURS

These dinosaurs also walked on two legs. They are best known, however, for having very tough skulls!

CERATOPSIANS

These plant-eating dinosaurs had large eye-catching frills on their heads that could be used for protection. Their frills also helped them to keep warm in cold weather.

ORNITHOPODS

Ornithopods included several dinosaurs with duck-like beaks and crests on their heads. They were all plant-eaters rather than meat-eaters.

SAUROPODS

Sauropods included some of the largest dinosaurs to ever walk the Earth! They are easy to identify because they all had very long necks and tails, with incredibly small heads in comparison.

STEGOSAURS

Stegosaurs walked on four legs. Their most iconic features are the incredibly tough plates that ran across their backs and provided them with protection.

ANKYLOSAURS

Like stegosaurs, ankylosaurs had protective plates across their bodies. Ankylosaurs, however, had much shorter legs and often had tails that were shaped like clubs.

PTEROSAURS

These reptiles were close cousins of the dinosaurs and were the first animals after insects to develop the ability to fly. The very biggest had a similar wingspan to a small plane!

DEADLY DINOSAURS

The most ferocious dinosaurs of all were those with incredible features that helped them track and catch prey. Some had terribly sharp teeth and claws for grabbing onto their victims. Others were deadly because they were speedy or stealthy, had super keen senses, or hunted as a pack. The dinosaurs in this book were not to be messed with!

Tyrannosaurus rex

The most famous dinosaur of all, Tyrannosaurus rex was also one of the biggest land **predators** to have ever walked on Earth! It had huge teeth – bigger than any other dinosaur – which were perfect for crunching through skin and bone.

PRONUNCIATION: tie-RAN-oh-SORE-us rex

DIET: Carnivore

TIME PERIOD: Late **Cretaceous**

SIZE	4 of 5
SPEED	3 of 5
DEADLY RATING	5 of 5

Deinonychus

Deinonychus's name means "terrible claw" – it's easy to see why! This dinosaur had an extra large claw on each foot, which it would have used to latch onto and pin its **prey** against the ground. It is also likely that it had feathers!

PRONUNCIATION: dye-NON-ick-us	**SIZE**						
DIET: Carnivore	**SPEED**						
TIME PERIOD: Early Cretaceous	**DEADLY RATING**						

Spinosaurus

Spinosaurus is the largest meat-eating animal to ever live! It hunted in and around water, using its long snout to catch any unsuspecting fish or other marine creatures. Its nostrils were far back on its head, which meant it could breathe even when partly underwater.

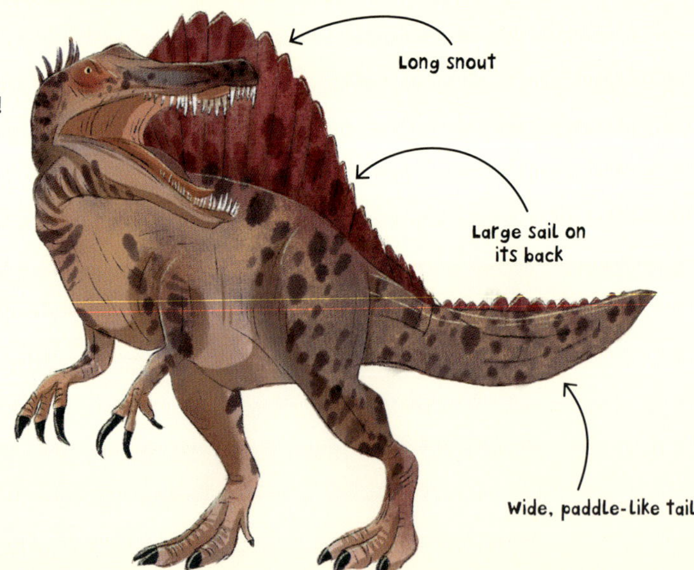

PRONUNCIATION: SPINE-oh-SORE-us	**SIZE**						
DIET: Carnivore	**SPEED**						
TIME PERIOD: Late Cretaceous	**DEADLY RATING**						

Allosaurus

Allosaurus was one of the fiercest dinosaurs of its time! Nothing was safe from this large predator, even other dinosaurs! With its backward-curving teeth, once Allosaurus gripped its prey there was no way to escape.

PRONUNCIATION: AL-oh-sore-us

DIET: Carnivore

TIME PERIOD: Late **Jurassic**

SIZE

SPEED

DEADLY RATING

Compsognathus

Compsognathus may have been no bigger than a chicken, but what it lacked in size it made up for in speed! Its strong back legs propelled it across the ground incredibly quickly when chasing prey.

PRONUNCIATION: komp-sog-NATH-us

DIET: Carnivore

TIME PERIOD: Late Jurassic

SIZE

SPEED

DEADLY RATING

Coelophysis

Coelophysis was one of the earliest known carnivorous dinosaurs. It had **hollow** bones that made it very light on its feet, and forward-facing eyes that gave it excellent vision. This, mixed with its sharp claws and teeth, made it a very deadly predator.

PRONUNCIATION: seel-OH-fie-sis

DIET: Carnivore

TIME PERIOD: Late **Triassic**

SIZE

SPEED

DEADLY RATING

Carcharodontosaurus

This dinosaur had many similarities to Tyrannosaurus rex (page 9). It was as tall as a double-decker bus with small arms and as many as 60 teeth. But Carcharodontosaurus and T. rex lived in different parts of the world at different times, so these two giants would never have met.

PRONUNCIATION: kar-KAR-o-don-toe-sore-us

DIET: Carnivore

TIME PERIOD: Late Cretaceous

SIZE  

SPEED

DEADLY RATING 

Helicoprion

This shark-like creature had a **unique** spiral-shaped lower jaw called a "whorl"! It would have acted like a saw, allowing Helicoprion to eat both hard- and soft-bodied prey.

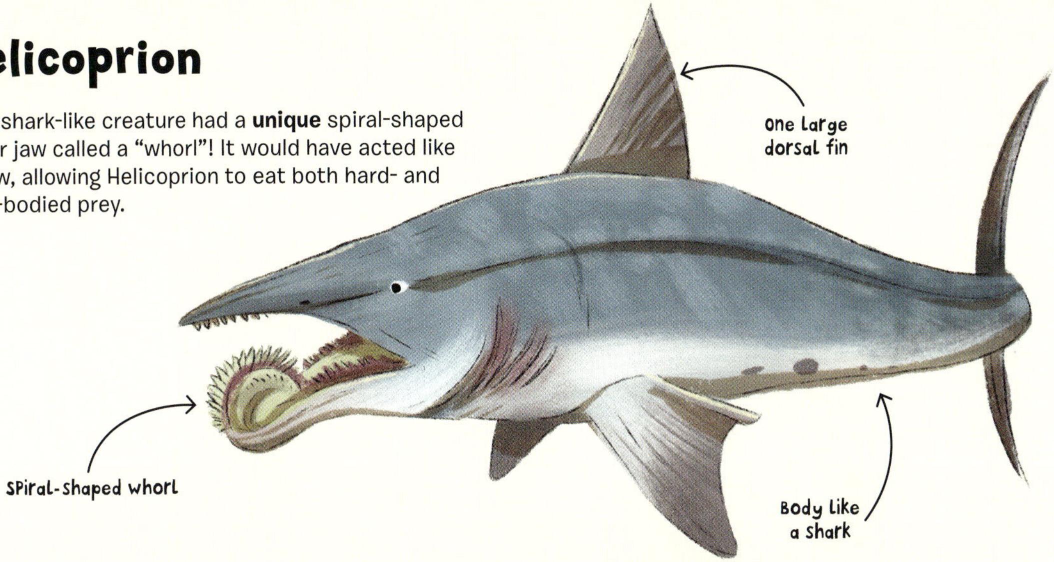

One large dorsal fin

Spiral-shaped whorl

Body like a shark

PRONUNCIATION: hel-ee-KO-pree-on

DIET: Carnivore

TIME PERIOD: Early **Permian**

SIZE

SPEED

DEADLY RATING

Microraptor

Microraptor is one of the smallest dinosaurs ever found! Despite having four wings, it isn't certain if it could fly properly. Instead, it likely jumped from branches high up in the trees and glided through the air in search of insects, small **mammals**, and fish to eat.

PRONUNCIATION: MIKE-roe-rap-tor

DIET: Carnivore

TIME PERIOD: Early Cretaceous

worked in teams

Stenonychosaurus

Fast and with great vision, Stenonychosaurus was a very smart dinosaur. It had the largest brain relative to its size of any dinosaur, and it is thought that it hunted in groups to take down much larger prey! For many years scientists thought that its fossils were from another dinosaur called Troodon. But they now think that most of those fossils did in fact belong to Stenonychosaurus!

Large eyes

Long fingers

Slender legs

PRONUNCIATION: sten-oh-NYE-ko-sore-us

DIET: Omnivore

TIME PERIOD: Late Cretaceous

SIZE	2/5
SPEED	4/5
DEADLY RATING	3/5

Velociraptor

Even though it was covered in feathers, Velociraptor's short arms meant it couldn't actually fly! Instead, the feathers were likely used to shield itself or its nests from the cold. Light and **agile**, Velociraptor chased after its prey and used its long claws to pin them down.

Long, stiff tail

Thick arm feathers

Sharp claws on each foot

PRONUNCIATION: vel-OSS-i-rap-tor	**SIZE** ●●○○○
DIET: Carnivore	**SPEED** ●●●●○
TIME PERIOD: Late Cretaceous	**DEADLY RATING** ●●●○○

Liopleurodon

These giant marine reptiles likely had no predators! They were at the top of the **food chain** and used their large flippers to push themselves through the water in search of large fish and other marine reptiles to feast on.

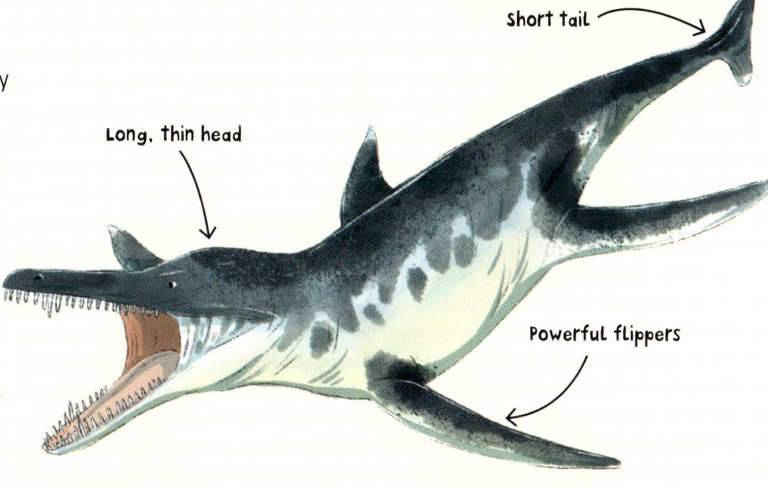

PRONUNCIATION: lee-oh-PLUR-oh-don

DIET: Omnivore

TIME PERIOD: Mid to late Jurassic

SIZE

SPEED

DEADLY RATING

Albertosaurus

This dinosaur was large and powerful. It is often compared to Tyrannosaurus rex (page 9) and shares many similarities, including its short arms, strong bite, and large skull. It is possible that they hunted in groups – how terrifying!

PRONUNCIATION: al-BERT-oh-SORE-russ

DIET: Carnivore

TIME PERIOD: Late Cretaceous

SIZE

SPEED

DEADLY RATING

Dakotaraptor

Dakotaraptor is one of the largest feathered theropods ever found! But despite its size and weight, it was still very agile, fast, and good at jumping. This made it a very intimidating predator.

PRONUNCIATION: da-KOH-ta-rap-tor

DIET: Carnivore

TIME PERIOD: Cretaceous

SIZE

SPEED

DEADLY RATING

Ceratosaurus

Ceratosaurus had a sharp horn on its head and small pieces of bony armor running along its back. It seems that this was quite a rare dinosaur, and a lot about it is still a mystery. Scientists still don't know what its horn was actually used for!

PRONUNCIATION: sir-AT-oh-SORE-us

DIET: Carnivore

TIME PERIOD: Late Jurassic

SIZE

SPEED

DEADLY RATING

Giganotosaurus

As its name suggests, Giganotosaurus was gigantic! Not only was it very tall, it was also very fast and preyed on other large dinosaurs. There is also evidence of it living in family groups.

PRONUNCIATION: gig-an-OH-toe-SORE-us	**SIZE**
DIET: Carnivore	**SPEED**
TIME PERIOD: Early Cretaceous	**DEADLY RATING**

Plesiosaurus

These marine reptiles had four large flippers. It is believed that the front pair were used for pushing Plesiosaurus through the water, while the back pair were to help with direction. They moved up and down rather than from side to side, making Plesiousaurus's style of swimming very unusual!

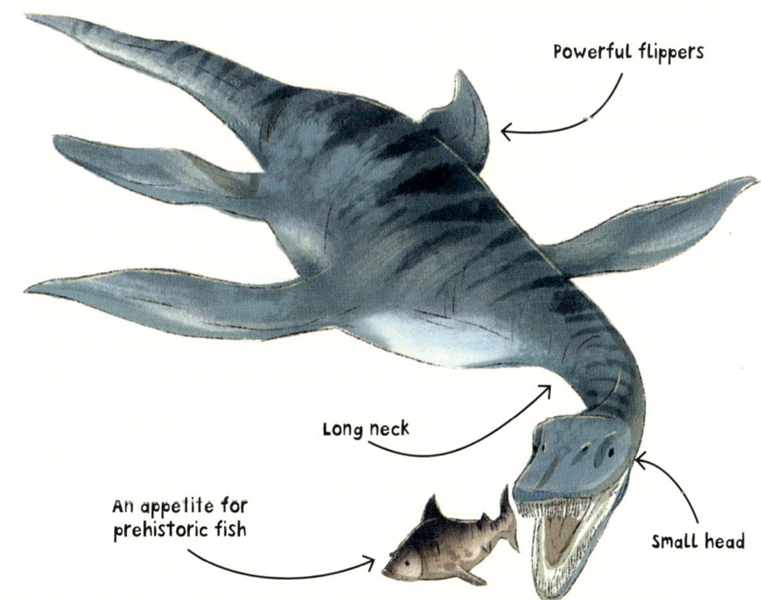

PRONUNCIATION: PLE-see-oh-SORE-us	**SIZE**
DIET: Carnivore	**SPEED**
TIME PERIOD: Jurassic	**DEADLY RATING**

Rugops

Rugops is a very mysterious dinosaur to science. The only fossil ever found of it is a skull! It was likely that it had scales on its head and possibly the rest of its body. It may also have been a **scavenger**, picking up the scraps left behind by other hunters.

PRONUNCIATION: ROO-gops

DIET: Carnivore

TIME PERIOD: Late Cretacious

SIZE

SPEED

DEADLY RATING

Dilophosaurus

Dilophosaurus featured two distinctive crests on the top of its head, made from the same material as human hair and nails! Despite its large size, this dinosaur is thought to have been fast, and had sharp claws that it used to catch and hold onto its prey.

PRONUNCIATION: die-LOAF-oh-sore-us

DIET: Carnivore

TIME PERIOD: Early Jurassic

SIZE   

SPEED

DEADLY RATING   

Baryonyx

This dinosaur's head looked a lot like a crocodile's! Its teeth were cone-shaped rather than blade-shaped, and it had an amazingly big claw at the end of each arm that it used to hook slippery fish out of the water.

PRONUNCIATION: bah-ree-ON-icks	**SIZE**	● ● ● ● ○
DIET: Carnivore	**SPEED**	● ● ● ○ ○
TIME PERIOD: Early Cretaceous	**DEADLY RATING**	● ● ● ○ ○

Carnotaurus

Carnotaurus was a fearsome-looking dinosaur with two prominent horns on its head. Rather than being used for hunting prey, these horns were likely used for ramming or shoving one another. But despite its intimidating face, Carnotaurus had tiny arms!

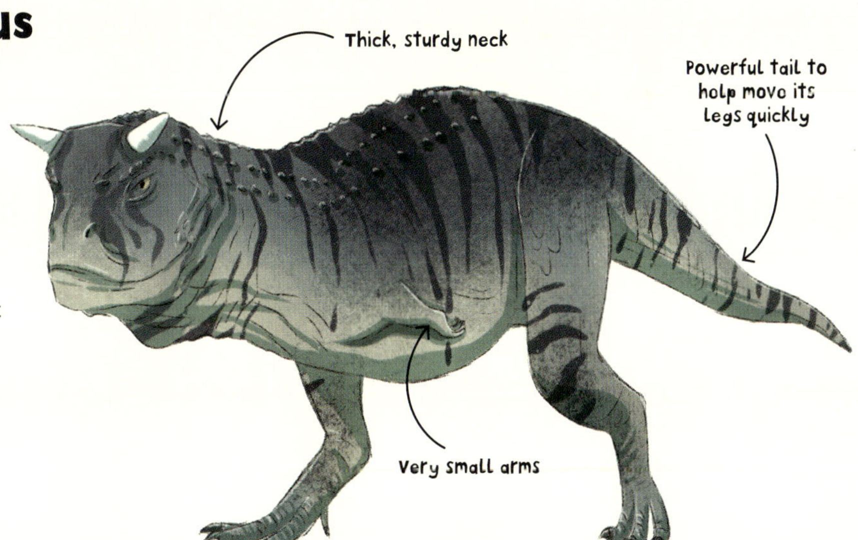

PRONUNCIATION: kar-noh-TORE-us	**SIZE**	● ● ● ○ ○ 
DIET: Carnivore	**SPEED**	● ● ● ● ○
TIME PERIOD: Late Cretaceous	**DEADLY RATING**	● ● ● ○ ○  

Majungasaurus

Majungasaurus grew a new set of teeth every two months! This is the fastest growth rate of any meat-eating dinosaur. This suggests it didn't just eat the meat of its prey, but it chomped on their bones too!

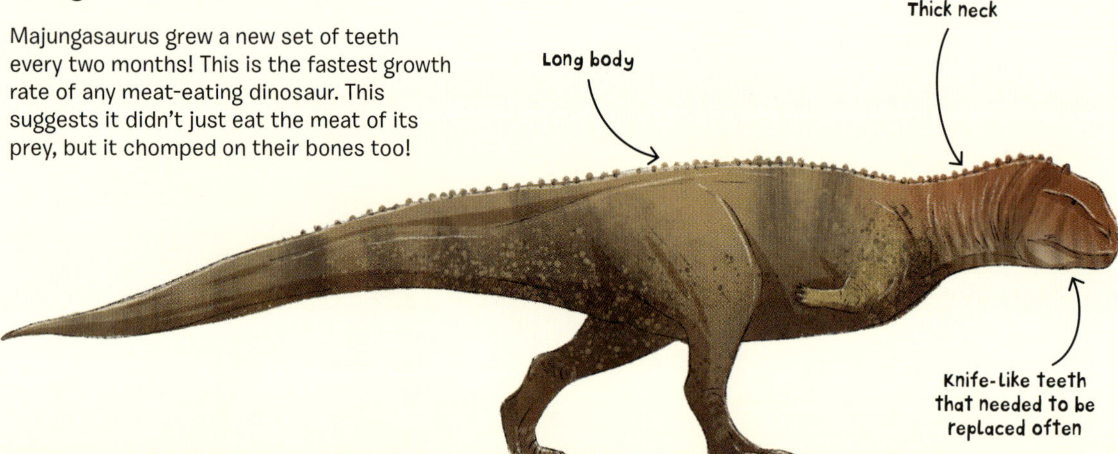

PRONUNCIATION: mah-joon-gah-SORE-us	SIZE
DIET: Carnivore	SPEED
TIME PERIOD: Late Cretaceous	DEADLY RATING

Sinornithosaurus

Even though it had feathers like a modern-day bird, this dinosaur couldn't fly. It was, however, good at leaping. Its long tail helped it to keep its balance as it jumped from spot to spot either to chase prey or to escape from predators.

PRONUNCIATION: sine-or-NITH-oh-SORE-us	SIZE	   
DIET: Carnivore	SPEED	
TIME PERIOD: Early Cretaceous	DEADLY RATING	  

Dracorex

Even though its name means "dragon king", Dracorex was very much a dinosaur. Its skull featured multiple horns and spikes. Because it was a **herbivore**, these wouldn't have been used to catch prey. Instead, they would have been used to help Dracorex defend itself from predators.

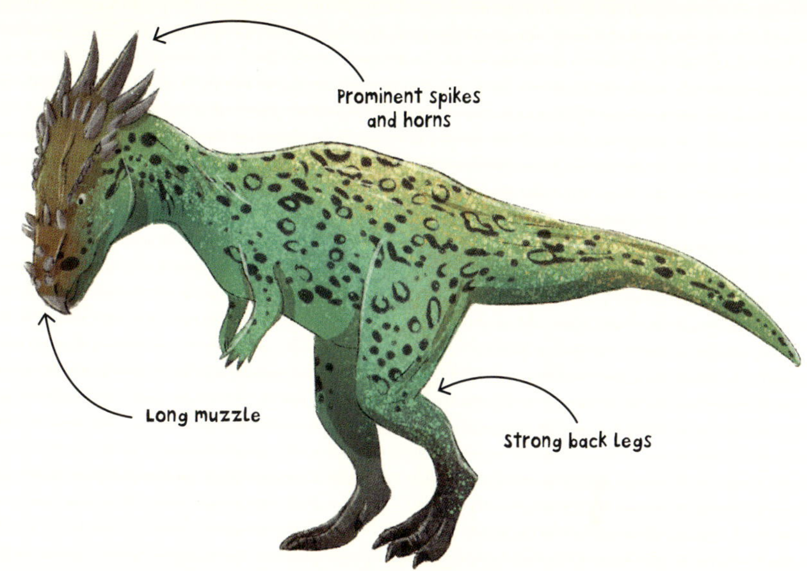

PRONUNCIATION: dray-KO-rex	**SIZE**	
DIET: Herbivore	**SPEED**	
TIME PERIOD: Late Cretaceous	**DEADLY RATING**	

Mapusaurus

Mapusaurus was one of the largest meat-eating dinosaurs ever. Scientists have found evidence that suggests it hunted and lived in groups, meaning it would have been able to take on and overpower even the very biggest plant-eating dinosaurs.

PRONUNCIATION: mah-puh-SORE-us	**SIZE**	  
DIET: Carnivore	**SPEED**	
TIME PERIOD: Late Cretaceous	**DEADLY RATING**	 

DID YOU KNOW?

What more is there to know about these deadly dinos? Let's take a look at some amazing facts and find out!

The smallest carnivorous dinosaur was the Compsognathus. It was as small as a chicken and mostly ate other small animals.

The T. rex had 50 to 60 teeth, and each tooth was as big as a banana. A Hadrosaurus, however, is thought to have had 960 smaller teeth!

Hadrosaurus

T. rex

The Spinosaurus is the longest carnivorous dinosaur currently known. Fossils suggest it was three times the length of an African elephant, and 20% heavier!

A Giganotosaurus could run faster than a T. rex, reaching speeds up to 20 miles per hour (32 km per hour).

Paleontologists and archaeologists have discovered up to 11,000 dinosaur fossils across the world so far but believe there are still millions left to find.

Many carnivorous dinosaurs are now thought to have had feathers, which may have been used to keep warm, **camouflage**, or show off to their friends.

DINO DISCOVERY!

Want to be a dino detective? Paleontologists dig up clues to learn about dinosaurs - and you can too!

What is a paleontologist?

A paleontologist is a scientist who looks for fossils - which could be old bones, teeth, and even footprints left behind by dinosaurs millions of years ago!

They dig very carefully so they don't break anything. Then, they study the fossils to figure out what dinosaurs looked like, how they lived, and what they ate.

Tools of the trade

Paleontologists don't use pirate shovels or giant machines. They use small tools, like:

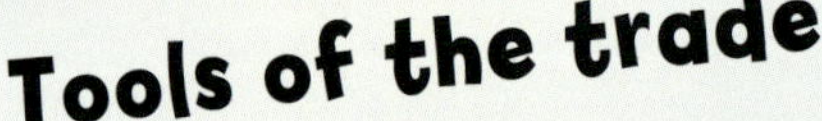

- A brush to gently clean off the dirt
- A little pick to chip away at rock
- A magnifying glass to look at tiny details
- A notebook to write down any discoveries

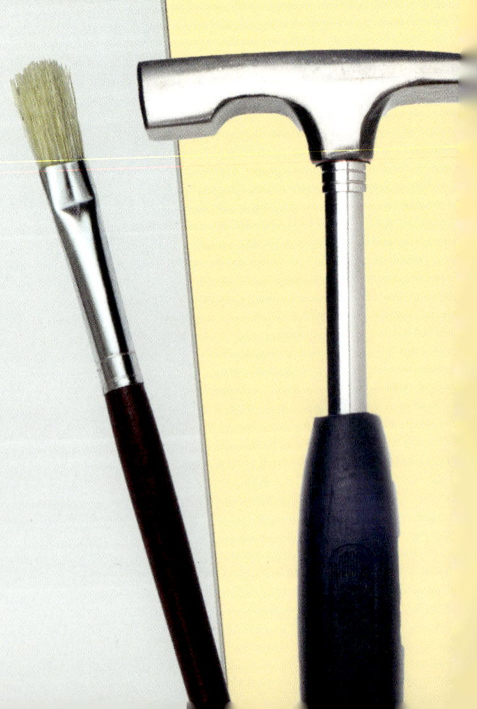

Let's play dino detective!

Imagine you find something hard in the dirt... It's a bone!
What do you do?

STEP 1: Dig carefully
Use a brush to clear the dirt!

STEP 2: Take notes
What shape is it? Big or small?

STEP 3: Ask questions
Which dino is this from?

STEP 4: Make a guess
Maybe it's a T. rex leg!

STEP 5: Compare it
Look at pictures of other dino bones to find a match.

WHICH DEADLY DINO IS THIS?

Follow the clues to uncover which meat-eating dinosaur you're thinking of! Start at the top and use YES or NO to follow the path.

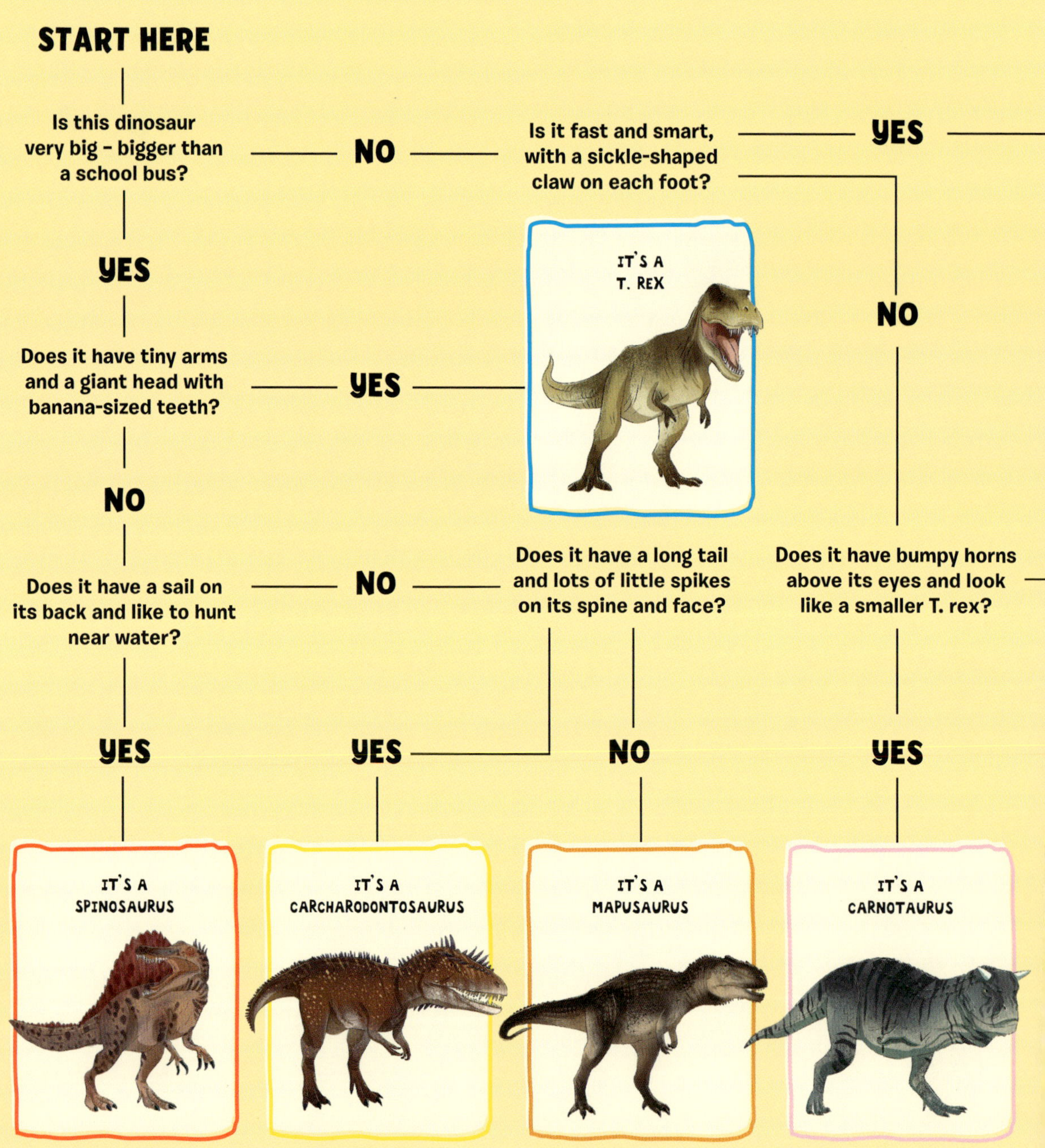

IT'S A COELOPHYSIS

NO

Is it bigger than a Velociraptor but still very fast?

YES

IT'S A DEINONYCHUS

NO

Does it hunt in packs and maybe even have feathers?

YES

IT'S A VELOCIRAPTOR

NO

IT'S A GIGANOTOSAURUS

PICK A DINOSAUR!

Choose one of the following dinosaurs - now, answer the questions to find them!

Carcharodontosaurus
(page 12)

Velociraptor
(page 16)

Carnotaurus
(page 21)

Mapusaurus
(page 23)

Spinosaurus
(page 10)

Deinonychus
(page 10)

Giganotosaurus
(page 19)

Coelophysis
(page 12)

T. rex
(page 9)

GLOSSARY

Agile – the ability to move very quickly and easily.

Asteroid – small, rocky objects that orbit the sun.

Carnivore – an animal that only eats meat.

Camouflage – a way animals hide by blending in with their surroundings.

Continents – huge pieces of land on Earth. For example, Africa and North America are different continents.

Cretaceous – a period of time that last from about 143 to 66 million years ago.

Extinct – a species of animals with no living members.

Food chain – the order in which different species eat each other to survive.

Fossils – the remains or impression of plants and animals that lived long ago.

Herbivore – an animal that only eats plants.

Hollow – something that has an empty space inside.

Jurassic – a period of time that lasted from about 201 to 143 million years ago.

Mammals – warm-blooded animals (including humans) that produce milk to feed their young.

Omnivore – an animal that eats both plants and meat.

Permian – a period of time that lasted from about 299 to 251 million years ago.

Predators – animals that hunt and kill other animals for food.

Prey – an animal that is hunted by other animals for food.

Reptiles – a group of cold-blooded animals, including snakes, lizards, crocodiles, and some types of dinosaurs.

Scavenger – an animal that eats animals that are dead instead of hunting for living animals to kill and eat.

Skeleton – the bony frame that supports and protects the body of a person or animal.

Triassic – a period of time that lasted from about 251 to 201 million years ago.

Unique – something that stands out and is completely different from everything else.

INDEX

ABOUT THE AUTHOR

Rosie Rowntree is a children's author living in the west of Cornwall. Sharing her love of learning through her writing, she is passionate about sparking curiosity in children as they begin to broaden their horizons and learn about their surroundings - and beyond!

ABOUT THE ILLUSTRATOR

Marina Halak is a talented illustrator of children's books from Ukraine. Her stunning illustrations are inspired by her own childhood, children, nature, magical moments and fairy tales. Marina is also the illustrator behind the related series, *Dogs* and *Cats*.

Picture Credits:
(abbreviations: t=top, b=bottom, m=middle, l=left, r=right)

Shutterstock: 3DMI 26br; AKaiser 26bl; Autumn Sky Photography 27 (step 5); Digital_Lions 27 (step 4); Dotted Yeti 25bl; Elnur 27 (step 1); Evgeny Haritonov 27 (step 2); Frame Stock Footage 27 (step 3); Gorodenkoff 25mrl; Irina Gutyryak 27bl; Orla 24bl; Ortis 26br; palaeontologist natural 26tr; sergey Kolesnikov 24tl; Vladimir Bolokh 24mr; Warpaint 25tl.

Every effort has been made to trace the copyright holders, and we apologize in advance for any unintentional omissions. We would be pleased to insert the appropriate acknowledgments in any subsequent edition of this publication.